ITALY

ITALY

by A. M. Buckley

Content Consultant
Jacob Soll
Professor of History, Rutgers–Camden

CREDITS

Published by ABDO Publishing Company, 8000 West 78th Street, Edina, Minnesota 55439. Copyright © 2012 by Abdo Consulting Group, Inc. International copyrights reserved in all countries. No part of this book may be reproduced in any form without written permission from the publisher. The Essential Library™ is a trademark and logo of ABDO Publishing Company.

Printed in the United States of America,
North Mankato, Minnesota
062011
092011

Editor: Melissa York
Copy Editor: Susan M. Freese
Series design and cover production: Emily Love
Interior production: Kazuko Collins

About the Author: A. M. Buckley is an artist, writer, and children's book author based in Los Angeles, California. She has written several books for children, including the *Kids Yoga Deck*. She will never forget the magical experience of watching Venice wake up along its aged and watery avenues after arriving in the city at dawn as a young backpacker.

Library of Congress Cataloging-in-Publication Data
Buckley, A. M., 1968-
  Italy / by A. M. Buckley.
     p. cm. -- (Countries of the world)
  Includes bibliographical references and index.
  ISBN 978-1-61783-114-0
  1. Italy--Juvenile literature. I. Title.
  DG417.B77 2011
  945--dc23
                              2011020918

Cover: The Colosseum, Rome, Italy

TABLE OF CONTENTS

CHAPTER 1
A VISIT TO ITALY

As you bound off the train into the Roma Termini, or "Roman Terminal," the major train station in the capital of Italy, you feel ready to experience Rome, one of the world's oldest and most dramatic cities. In the airy station, you pass stylish Italians talking rapidly and energetically with traveling companions or into cell phones, matrons rounding up their children, and widows and nuns waiting patiently in their all-black attire. Among them are immigrants from northern Africa, eastern Europe, and Asia and visitors and business travelers from all over the world.

You make your way to the center of the city and stop in the Piazza Navona, one of Rome's many plazas, or city squares. Originally, the plaza was an arena for the ancient Romans, and it later housed a large public market for three centuries. In what is now an immense and impressive city square, you see Italians visiting with one

Italians call their country Italia, short for the official name, Repubblica Italiana.

A view of the Tiber River in Rome with Saint Peter's Basilica in the background

THE CATS OF ROME

In Rome, there are cats around nearly every corner. They lurk at the edges of extravagant fountains, prowl beneath ancient stone arches, and loiter on the edges of crowded plazas and busy cafés. The cats of Rome are not ordinary house cats—tame and friendly—but a seemingly timeless breed of urban cats—tough, proud, and fearless. "The oldest Romans are the cats," writes author Michael Sheridan in his book *Romans: Their Lives and Times*. He continues, "An old legend holds that the souls of dead generations inhabit the unkempt skeletons of the cats, so that in their eyes you see the very depths of antiquity."[1]

another over their morning espressos. You are surprised to see bands of cats lurking at the edges of the square, and you notice a few elderly women feeding them bits of spaghetti.

A walk just outside the plaza takes you to two of Rome's fantastic churches, graced with world-class art. Inside the Church of Sant'Agostino, you stand in front of a fresco created in 1512 by Raphael, one of only a few Italian artists famous enough to be known by a single name. You walk quietly through the elegant, arced hallways to see a painting made in 1604 by another Italian master, Caravaggio. In a Baroque church nearby, San Luigi dei Francesi, you marvel at a trio of paintings by this artist.

There are so many amazing sights to see that you must keep moving, aiming for the heart of the ancient city. Under the Mediterranean sunshine lie ruins of the 2,000-year-old Roman Empire, with fragments of ancient stone rising from the grass. You visit the Pantheon, a temple begun in 27 BCE and rebuilt between 118 and 128 CE by the emperor Hadrian to honor the Roman gods. Gazing up, you can hardly believe the immense dome has survived all these centuries. Making your way across the Forum, the heart of the ancient city, you arrive at the Colosseum. Here, surrounded by visitors from around the world, you can almost hear the roar of the gladiators fighting fiercely to the death.

Exhausted but exhilarated, you decide it's high time to indulge in some of Italy's famous cuisine. You head over to another of Rome's city squares, the Piazza di Spagna, or "Spanish Square," where you settle into a restaurant on the plaza for a delicious lunch. Enjoying your meal the

THE COLOSSEUM

Originally called the Flavian Amphitheater, the Roman Colosseum was built by the Roman emperor Vespasian. It took ten years to complete and was inaugurated in the year 80 CE with a day-and-night competition that lasted 100 days. Gladiators battled one another and prisoners were forced to fight for their lives against lions and other animals.

The Colosseum was not the largest of the Roman amphitheaters. That honor went to the 200,000-seat Circus Maximus, which used to hold chariot races nearby. Even so, the Colosseum could hold 50,000 people.[2] Three stories of arches define the outer walls. The arena has 80 doors to allow for the rapid entrance and exit of large crowds. Both a marvel of living history and a feat of architecture, the Colosseum is a major tourist attraction in Rome. The structure remains almost completely intact after more than 2,000 years.

Italian way, you take your time with each course—bread and olives, pasta and sauce, some meat or vegetables, and a plate of fruit and cheese.

Your stomach full, you wander over to the Scalinata della Trinità dei Monti, known as the "Spanish Steps," which has been a favorite spot for lounging and people watching since the eighteenth century. Romans and visitors alike relax on the steps, which feature successive flights of stairs interspersed with ramps like patios.

As you sit, you notice how beautifully dressed the Romans are as they make their way through the city. Whether turned out in luxurious designer wear or dressed more simply, each person has selected clothes with style and an eye for detail—from a brightly colored scarf to a polished pair of shoes.

Beyond the steps is yet another lovely church, and the trees in the plaza are in bloom. You walk down and through the streets to the famous Trevi Fountain. The largest of Rome's numerous fountains, it was designed by Italian Nicola Salvi and built in 1732. The scene it depicts is inspired by Roman lore: sea horses, one calm and one unruly, lead the way for Neptune, the Roman god of the sea. Following a time-honored custom, you fish a euro from your pocket and toss it into the fountain, ensuring that you will return yet again to the Eternal City to see more of its fabled sights.

The Trevi Fountain is the largest of Rome's world-famous fountains.

Political Boundaries of Italy

PASSION MEETS HISTORY

Rome has been the seat of a vast empire, one of many powerful city-states, the base of a fascist dictatorship, and a provincial city. Today, it is a thriving international metropolitan area, the seat of the Catholic Church, and the capital of Italy.

You took note of Rome's legacy of powerful popes and famous artists in the city's glorious cathedrals and renowned works of art. In the train station, you noticed a diversity of people. Indeed, Rome is home to Italians from all over the nation, as well as immigrants from Asia, northern Africa, and eastern Europe. And, of course, visitors travel to Rome from around the globe.

As you wandered along the enchanting streets of Rome, you marveled at the charm and style of the city's inhabitants. Italy is a

LA BELLA FIGURA

You may not hear Italians mention *la bella figura,* but you notice it in their manner of dress and interaction. The phrase, meaning "the beautiful figure," has come to be a trademark of the Italian way of life and culture. It means to look your best, which includes how you look and how you act and treat others. In Italian culture, it is important to put forth your best—to dress neatly with style and to treat others graciously.

La bella figura extends to many aspects of Italian culture, valuing poise, style, and manners. This can include selecting and giving the perfect gift, as well as receiving a gift with grace and kindness. Likewise, beauty and grace are part of setting a lovely table, serving locally grown foods and home-cooked meals, and showing the proper appreciation for such gestures.

nation of diverse regions, but the passionate, stylish, wise, and engaged manner of the Romans is typical of the national character. These qualities come together in the Italian lifestyle, with an emphasis on socializing with friends, family, and neighbors; enjoying good, local food; and paying attention to the design and style of daily life.

NORTH AND SOUTH

Rome is representative of Italy in many ways, but it also marks an economic division between the north and the south. Located near the middle of the country, Rome is the entry to the south, the area of the nation where the majority of Italians living in poverty reside. The north, home to the business capital of Milan, has more industry, better-paying jobs, and a higher standard of living than the south.

You spent time in baroque cathedrals and ancient arenas, admiring the art and architecture of Rome. From the handblown glass of Venice to the marble sculpture of Carrara, Italy has nurtured artists gifted in all forms of art. From castles nestled in the flowering hillsides of Umbria to the sleek fashion and business centers of Milan, beauty abounds in Italy.

With a history that stretches back thousands of years, Italy is, in many ways, a living museum. It has seen the rise and fall of a great empire and the competition of independent states. This peninsula jutting out into

The Leaning Tower of Pisa is one of Italy's many iconic buildings.

the Mediterranean Sea has been occupied by the French, the Spanish, and the Germans, among others. In fact, Italy did not become a unified nation until the middle of the nineteenth century. Relics of the country's religious, political, and artistic legacy can be seen in monuments to past leaders and relics of civilizations, in art and buildings, and in the attitude and style of the people.

"You may have the universe if I may have Italy."[3]

—*Giuseppe Verdi, Italian composer, from the opera Attila*

[SNAPSHOT]

Official name: Italian Republic (Italian: Repubblica Italiana)

Capital city: Rome

Form of government: republic

Title of leader: president (head of state); prime minister (head of government)

Currency: euro

Population (July 2011 est.): 61,016,804
World rank: 23

Size: 116,348 square miles (301,340 sq km)
World rank: 71

Language: Italian

Official religion: none; Roman Catholicism, 90 percent

Per capita GDP (2010, US dollars): $30,700
World rank: 43

CHAPTER 2

GEOGRAPHY: FROM THE MOUNTAINS TO THE SEAS

Italy, located in southern Europe, is comprised of 116,348 square miles (301,340 sq km) of mountainous land that roughly forms the shape of a boot.[1] Surrounded on three sides by the Mediterranean Sea, Italy has 4,971 miles (8,000 km) of coastline, varying from low, flat beaches to tall, jagged cliffs along the sea.[2]

Northern Italy is crossed from east to west by a mountain range called the Italian Alps, a large range dotted with more than 1,000 glaciers.[3] The westerly Alpine peaks are the highest and include the 14,692 foot (4,478 m) Monte Cervino, or Matterhorn.[4] On the eastern side, the Alpi Dolomitiche, or Dolomites mountain group, feature lower but dramatically jagged peaks. The foothills are dotted with lakes.

Italy's coast varies from rocky cliffs to sandy beaches.

The Italian Alps are rugged and capped with snow.

The north is also home to Italy's largest river, the Po, which extends for 405 miles (652 km) and creates a fertile plain across northern and central Italy.[5] A second mountain range, the Appennino, or Apennines, stretches from north to south and dominates the majority of the mountainous Italian peninsula.

Italy is located on a long fault line—a vulnerable area of the earth's crust—that extends from north to south. The land is especially prone to earthquakes. Italy also has six active volcanoes.

The country also includes the islands of Sicily in the south and Sardinia in the west, plus many smaller islands. To the north, Italy shares borders with France, Switzerland, Austria, and Slovenia. Peninsular Italy is surrounded by four regions of the Mediterranean Sea: the Ligurian Sea on the west, the Adriatic Sea on the east, and the Ionian and Tyrrhenian Seas on the south.

Within its territory, Italy has two sovereign

DESTRUCTIVE EARTHQUAKES

Minor earthquakes occur several times a year in Italy. Powerful quakes are less common but have caused serious damage throughout the years.

In 1693, earthquakes killed approximately 60,000 people in Catania and Sicily and 93,000 in Naples. Nearly a century later, in 1783, another powerful earthquake struck southern Italy, killing approximately 50,000 people in the region of Calabria.[6]

More dangerous earthquakes rocked Italy during the twentieth century. On December 28, 1908, the most powerful quake ever recorded in Europe hit the Strait of Messina, an area separating Sicily from Calabria, and killed an estimated 200,000 people. Seven years later, in 1915, a second powerful quake killed 30,000 people and destroyed the town of Avezzano. A 1976 earthquake struck the northeastern region of Friuli, killing nearly 100 people and leaving 70,000 without homes, and a 1980 earthquake in Eboli killed more than 2,700 people in villages in and around the city of Naples and injured more than 7,500.[7]

The most recent major earthquake to strike Italy hit L'Aquila, a medieval city east of Rome, in Abruzzi on April 6, 2009. The 6.3-magnitude quake killed almost 300 people and severely damaged the city's buildings and infrastructure.[8]

ITALIAN VOLCANOES

Italy has three active volcanoes. The first, Stromboli, is located on the west coast, right above the "toe" of the boot. The second, Mount Etna, is on the island of Sicily, southwest of the main peninsula. The third, Mount Vesuvius, is located near the city of Naples. Vesuvius erupted in 79 CE, destroying the nearby towns of Pompeii and Herculaneum.

states. The tiny nation of the Vatican lies within Rome, and a very small country, San Marino, lies in northern Italy near Switzerland.

REGIONS AND TERRITORIES

Italy's geography can be divided into three main areas: the alpine mountains of the north, the flat Po River valley in the north, and the long, mountainous peninsula that makes up the majority of the country. The country is more than 75 percent mountainous.[9]

Today, roads crisscross Italy, making travel and communication easier, but in earlier times, the mountains created geographic boundaries and led, in part, to the creation of strong regional and cultural identities. Since Italy became a unified nation late in the nineteenth century, these regions have been organized under a centralized government, but they still retain their distinct cultural identities. Italy is divided into 15 regions and five autonomous regions, which, although part of Italy, are somewhat independent.

Geography of Italy

A FLOATING CITY

The city of Venice, capital of Veneto in northeastern Italy, is one of the nation's primary cultural and artistic centers. It is also one of 48 sites in Italy chosen by the United Nations Educational, Scientific, and Cultural Organization (UNESCO) as a World Heritage site. Venice has a long history, dating back to the fifth century, and a unique geography, as it is situated on 118 small islands in a lagoon.[10]

Since the streets in Venice are waterways, no cars can be found in the city. Instead, boats are used to carry people, mail, and everything else through Venice. People ride on public ferries or on a special form of long rowboat called a gondola, in which a gondolier stands up to row.

Venice was once an important port and one of the most prosperous city-states on the Italian peninsula. By the eleventh century, the city had grown into a massive maritime power. Over the centuries, Venice has remained a uniquely water-based city. It has attracted artists, writers, poets, and architects and is today home to many famous works of art and a number of extraordinary buildings.

The capital of Italy, Rome, is located in the region of Latium, which begins the southern area of the country. The industrial capital is Milan, in the northern region of Lombardy. The home of Italy's long artistic legacy is the city of Florence in Tuscany. Venice, in the region of Veneto, is an ancient city built on waterways.

TEMPERATURE AND CLIMATE

Italy is normally equated with warm, sunny weather. Indeed, much of the country is sunny from mid-May through October and graced with humid breezes. But spring can become chilly. Winters are

Gondolas navigate the waterways of Venice.

	Alpine Tundra
	Arid Steppe, Cold
	Temperate, Dry and Hot Summer
	Temperate, Dry and Warm Summer
	Temperate, No Dry Season, Hot Summer
	Temperate, No Dry Season, Warm Summer
	Cold, No Dry Season, Warm Summer
	Cold, No Dry Season, Cold Summer

Trento

Udine

Milan Verona

Venice

Genoa

Ligurian Sea

Bologna

Florence

Ancona

Adriatic Sea

Pescara

Rome

Bari

Naples

Taranto

Gulf of Taranto

Tyrrhenian Sea

Cagliari

Cosenza

Mediterranean Sea Palermo Messina

Ionian Sea

NORTH
↑

Climate of Italy

AVERAGE TEMPERATURES AND RAINFALL

Region (City)	Average January Temperature Minimum/Maximum	Average July Temperature Minimum/Maximum	Average Rainfall January/July
Po Valley and North Italian Plain (Milan)	32/41°F (0/5°C)	68/84°F (20/29°C)	1.7/2.5 inches (4.4/6.4 cm)
Central (Rome)	41/52°F (5/11°C)	68/86°F (20/30°C)	2.8/0.59 inches (7.1/1.5 cm)
The Italian Islands (Palermo)	41/52°F (8/16°C)	68/86°F (21/30°C)	2.8/0.1 Inches (7.1/0.2 cm)[12]

cold and rainy in most of Italy and even snowy in the north. In the fall, thunderstorms are common.

In northern Italy, where the mountains are higher than 10,000 feet (3,000 m), temperatures are cold in the winter and rainy in the summer with frequent thunderstorms.[11] The lower elevations of the mountains are slightly warmer, but overall, the weather is quite cold with heavy winter snows.

INDEPENDENT REGIONS OF ITALY

Italy has five independent regions that have their unique status due to historical and cultural factors. Three of these regions lie in the northern part of Italy, and each has linguistic and cultural ties to another country. In the Valle d'Aosta, located high in the Italian Alps, French was once the main language and remains so for some inhabitants. The second region, Trentino–Alto Adige, is divided between the Italian-speaking Trentino and the German-speaking Alto Adige, which was once a part of Austria. The final region, Friuli–Venezia Giulia, was once part of Yugoslavia.

Italy's two remaining independent regions are islands to the south and west. Sardinia and Sicily have long been independent due to their geographic separation from the peninsula.

Below the mountains, in the valley that surrounds the Po River, the climate features regular rainfall throughout the year, as well as hot summers and cold winters. Summers in the north are comparable to those in the sunny south, but northern winters are marked by fog, frost, and snow.

The central and southern regions of Italy have the most typical Mediterranean climate, although this varies from the coastal regions to the mountainous interior. Even though the coasts are warm throughout the year, winters are chilly in the mountainous interior, and snow is common at higher elevations. Coastal winters are mild, and summers are generally hot and dry. Italy's west coast receives more rainfall, on average, than its east coast. The mildest winters and sunniest conditions overall can be found in the southernmost regions of the peninsula and on the islands of Sicily and Sardinia.

Toscana, or Tuscany, is a region of picturesque rolling hills and vast, beautiful countryside.

CHAPTER 3

ANIMALS AND NATURE: A THRIVING PENINSULA

The unofficial national animal of Italy is the Italian wolf. The wolf is particularly important to Italy because it figures prominently in the legendary founding of Rome. Early in the twentieth century, the wolf faced extinction, and by the 1970s, only 100 or so were left in Italy. Thanks to intensive efforts to save the animal, there were 500 to 1,000 wolves in the country by 2007, living mostly in the Alps.[1]

Along with the wolves, the situation has improved for the lynx and the brown bear. Bears now roam free in northern Italy, although most reside in national parks.

Scientists debate whether the Italian wolf is a subspecies of gray wolf or a species of its own.

The Italian wolf, also called the European or Apennine wolf, is Italy's unofficial national animal.

Common mammals in Italy are deer, ibex, mountain goats, wildcats, hedgehogs, and rabbits.

The wide variety of birds in Italy includes raptors, such as the golden eagle and the peregrine falcon, as well as various types of swallows and partridges. The islands along Italy's coasts provide nesting places for a diversity of birds. And an area in Tuscany, in northwestern Italy, is a major migratory path through the Mediterranean for a number of birds.

Many fish swim in the waters that surround peninsular Italy, including swordfish, tuna, dolphins, and white sharks. Otters can be spotted off the southwest coast, and the very rare monk seal can be seen from time to time near Sardinia.

PLANT LIFE

Because people have built permanent communities in Italy for so many centuries, most of the land that was once forested is now covered in fields, orchards, towns, and cities.

ROMULUS AND REMUS

In Roman mythology, a pair of twins named Romulus and Remus were born to a priestess named Rhea Silvia and the Roman god Mars. The brothers were abandoned at birth and soon discovered by a female wolf that protected, fed, and nurtured them until a human couple found and adopted them. As grown men, the twins chose the spot where the wolf had fed them as the site for a new city. Misfortune befell the pair once again during the construction of the city, when Romulus killed Remus in a sibling rivalry. After the city was completed, the remaining brother named it for himself, and Rome began its long history.

Ibex in Gran Paradiso National Park, Valle d'Aosta, Italy

ENDANGERED SPECIES IN ITALY

According to the International Union for Conservation of Nature (IUCN), Italy is home to the following numbers of species that are categorized by the organization as Critically Endangered, Endangered, or Vulnerable:

Mammals	7
Birds	8
Reptiles	4
Amphibians	9
Fishes	42
Mollusks	30
Other Invertebrates	47
Plants	27
Total	174[2]

The plant life in the majority of the country consists of Mediterranean plants, which includes a variety of evergreen trees. The main three types in Italy are the ilex, or evergreen oak, plus the cork and the pine. Ancient forests still grow in some of the more isolated regions, such as the cork forests of Sicily and Sardinia and the ilex and oak forests in parts of Tuscany, Umbria, and Sardinia.

Cypress and olive trees were imported to Italy many centuries ago and are now common throughout the countryside. Herbs, such as lavender, rosemary, and thyme, and shrubs, including juniper and heather, grow throughout much of the country. In

Cypress trees are a distinctive feature of Italian landscape.

the spring, orchids and other flowers bloom at the base of this varied vegetation.

ENVIRONMENTAL PROTECTION

In recent years, Italy has focused on environmental protection. As a result, conditions for the natural environment have improved. The primary threats to the environment include smog and air pollution in the cities, particularly in the industrialized north, and waste disposal.

BEACHSIDE BUILDING

The island of Sardinia is famous for its beautiful beaches. However, these stunning coastlines are vulnerable to construction. In 2004, the regional president of Sardinia, Renato Soru, tried to save the island's beaches by passing legislation that banned new building within 1.2 miles (2 km) of the Sardinian coast.[3] But builders and critics opposed the law so strongly that Soru was voted out of office. His replacement changed the law so construction could continue as before.

The large number of cars in Italy contributes to smog, and efforts have been made to promote bicycling in order to curb this pollution. Local efforts to curb pollution include a charge levied by the city of Milan for congestion and a bicycle-sharing plan introduced by the city of Rome. Nationally, Italy has made an effort to reduce its dependency on oil and gas to curb harmful emissions. In 2009, the government

Nature reserves and national parks conserve the habitats of Italy's endangered animals, such as the griffon vulture.

made a commitment to build four nuclear power plants as an alternative energy source.

Waste disposal has been another source of concern for Italy. The country lacks sufficient incinerators for trash and does not have enough space in landfills. Italy's third-largest city, Naples, has especially suffered from problems with waste management. While political battles rage over solutions to the problem, waste continues to pile up, causing concerns for both health and the environment.

Italy is home to 30 endangered and 19 critically endangered animal species.

Increasing construction, primarily for the tourism industry, also poses a threat to Italy's environment, eroding vulnerable land along the coast. While conservationists aim to limit building and save the coasts, the construction industry continues its work. Although many of Italy's beaches have been harmed by construction, clean beaches remain in the areas of southern Puglia, Calabria, Sardinia, and Sicily.

Hunting is popular in Italy, and the strong hunting lobby prevents the government from passing stronger hunting laws. Conservationists argue that stronger restrictions are necessary to protect key species, especially migratory birds.

During the twentieth century, 14 species of animals became extinct in Italy, including the sea eagle, the alpine lynx, and the black vulture.[4]

PARKS AND PRESERVES

To prevent the extinction of more species, Italy has introduced legislation to protect vulnerable animals. Conservation efforts have aided some animals. In addition to wolves, bears, and lynx, animals that have been assisted in this effort include golden eagles, griffon vultures, and bearded vultures.

The Italian government passed laws to protect animals and created national parks and reserves, and the Italian people have also acted to preserve their nation's ecology. Legambiente, one of the primary nonprofit organizations for protecting and conserving the natural environment, was founded in 1980. This organization emphasizes local efforts and sustainable practices.

Italy has 24 national parks and 400 nature reserves, wetlands, and

GARGANO'S SEA-CARVED CAVES

One of Italy's many beautiful national parks lies in the region of Gargano in southeast Italy, in what can be considered the heel of the peninsula's boot. With rounded-top mountains rising up from the brilliant blue sea, Gargano is a natural wonder. Over the centuries, crashing waves have carved the mountains into caves and grottoes, which serve as homes for a variety of birds and marine life. A brief trip inland will take visitors to one of Italy's most ancient forests. The park is also known for its many varieties of orchids. And just off the coast lie the Tremeti Islands.

natural parks. The parks cover approximately 5 percent of the country's total land area.[5] The beautiful parks of Italy include natural wonders from granite peaks, rocky plateaus, and crystal lakes to dramatic coastlines and green seas, terraced hillsides and flowering meadows, rocky cliffs and limestone grottoes, and even live volcanoes.

In addition to its parks and nature reserves, Italy has 45 sites deemed significant by UNESCO as World Heritage sites. Italy has more of these sites than any other country in the world. These include the Dolomites in the north, the Amalfi coast in southwestern Italy, the city of Verona in northern Italy, and Vatican City, a tiny sovereign nation located within the boundaries of Rome.

Italy has three World Heritage sites chosen for their natural value and 45 for their cultural value.

The Dolomites Nature Reserve within the Dolomites mountains in northeast Italy

CHAPTER 4
HISTORY: AN INFLUENTIAL PAST

Evidence shows that human ancestors lived throughout the Italian peninsula as far back as 700,000 BCE. They hunted wild animals and did not build permanent homes. By 2000 BCE, modern humans had formed agricultural settlements.

The first major civilization to develop was the Etruscan society. Rising from the many tribes in the region, the Etruscans began gathering strength in the seventh century BCE and grew into a powerful civilization. By the sixth century BCE, the Etruscans dominated the majority of the Italian peninsula. Etruria, as the Etruscan territory was called, was organized into city-states, or small self-governing cities. The Etruscans developed language and currency and participated in farming, mining, and trading.

Etruscan sarcophagus used for burial, third century BCE

THE ROMAN REPUBLIC

The Roman Empire was the next major civilization to develop on the peninsula. It dominated the region for nearly 1,000 years and left an influential legacy around the world. According to legend, the city of Rome, which stands in the same place today, was founded in 753 BCE by a hero named Romulus. Archaeological evidence shows that Rome began as a small village and existed simultaneously to the Etruscan civilization for many years. But the Romans were tough warriors and fought the Etruscans, among others. As the Etruscan civilization lost power late in the fourth century BCE, the Romans grew stronger and eclipsed the older civilization.

Rome was known in Latin as the *caput mundi*, or "capital of the world."

Rome was organized into a republic with a partial democracy. Two elected consuls held military and political power. The Senate, whose members were appointed for life, advised the consuls. Although some officials were democratically elected, a small group of people regularly vied for position and control in the government. However, the vast majority of the people had little or no say over affairs of the state. By late in the third century BCE, the Roman Republic dominated the majority of the Italian peninsula. After Roman armies conquered the peninsula, they expanded in all directions, forming one of the largest empires in history.

The Forum was once the center of the Roman world.

ROMAN EMPERORS

One of the most famous Roman leaders was Gaius Julius Caesar. Born in 100 BCE, he was a general in the Roman army whose hunger for power led him all the way to the top of Roman society. Caesar's masterful but controversial reign ended when he was assassinated by a group of senators.

Caesar was succeeded by his lieutenant, Mark Antony, who took control of the eastern half of the Roman Empire, and by his great-nephew, Octavian, who took control of the western half. The pair of leaders went to war, first against Caesar's assassins and, eventually, against each other. Antony formed an alliance with Cleopatra, the queen of Egypt, and the two fell in love. Octavian invaded Egypt in 31 BCE, claiming it for Rome, and Antony and Cleopatra committed suicide.

By 27 BCE, Octavian had been assigned the title of *Augustus*, which means "Your Eminence," and given nearly complete control by the Senate as leader of the Roman Empire. Many historians consider Augustus Rome's greatest emperor. He undertook massive building projects and brought changes to nearly every aspect of Roman society, beginning a period of lasting peace and prosperity.

In the second and first centuries BCE, the Roman Republic was threatened by civil war, and a series of powerful men competed for control of the government. The turmoil culminated in the rule of Gaius Julius Caesar. He was assassinated by members of the Senate in 44 BCE because they feared he was becoming a king. Julius Caesar's great-nephew Octavian came to power in the confusion that resulted, defeating his enemies by 31 BCE. He took the name Augustus Caesar and he called himself *princeps*, or "the first of equals." He is considered the first emperor of Rome. From that point, the Senate was largely powerless, and Rome was ruled by emperors. At the height

of the Roman Empire,
in the second and third
centuries CE, the Romans
controlled a vast territory
that included half of Europe,
most of the Middle East, and
northern Africa.

Roman society
was characterized by an
interesting mix of borrowed
ideas and new innovations.
The Romans were powerful
warriors, shrewd politicians,
and inventive engineers.
The roads and the plumbing
system they developed
were the first of their kind,
and the impressive buildings
they constructed included

several innovations, including arches. Yet for the most part, the Romans'
religion and arts were adopted from the Greeks after the Romans
conquered that civilization. Greek gods were given Roman names, and
Roman artists borrowed heavily from Greek sculpture and painting.

A GREAT STATESMAN

Marcus Tullius Cicero was one of the most famous
writers and statesmen of ancient Rome. He wrote
numerous political speeches and essays on topics
as varied as ethics, friendship, and the gods. Cicero
initially gained fame for successfully prosecuting
a corrupt governor in 70 BCE. The precision and
skill of his many writings helped transform Latin
into the primary language of intellectual writings
for centuries. Cicero was twice banished from
Rome for his political beliefs, and he was killed by
Octavian and Mark Antony shortly after the death
of Julius Caesar.

AFTER THE FALL OF ROME

As the Roman Empire continued growing and expanding, a new religion was born—one that would have a strong effect on Italy's history and culture. Christianity began in the Middle East in the first century CE and spread throughout the region.

Initially, Christians were persecuted in the Roman Empire. However, the religion grew more prevalent and its members more powerful. In 312 CE, the Roman emperor Constantine converted to Christianity and made it the official religion of the Roman Republic.

By the fourth century, the Roman Empire had begun crumbling. In 395, it split into two parts: the East and the West. The West fell to northern invaders less than a century later, but the East, which became known as the Byzantine Empire, continued for centuries. The last Roman emperor, Romulus Augustulus, was defeated by a Germanic leader, Odoacer, in 476. This marked the end of the western Roman Empire. At this time, the Italian peninsula was divided between the Lombards, a Germanic tribe, and the Byzantine Empire.

The Byzantine Empire continued until the fifteenth century, when it was conquered by the Turks.

Meanwhile, Christianity in Europe flourished under the Roman Catholic Church, gaining political, social, and economic power.

Roman aqueducts are still standing in many locations around Europe, including at Pont du Gard in France.

The leader of the Catholic Church was the pope, and over time, the popes amassed power in Rome. In the eighth century, the Lombards began a march south to conquer papal lands. In 754–756, Pope Stephen II invited the Franks, led by Charlemagne, to invade Italy. Charlemagne's Carolingian Empire had absorbed much of northern Italy by 774. The popes gained independent power from the Byzantine Empire. In the meantime, the Lombards kept power in the southern region.

CITY-STATES

In the centuries following the fall of the Roman Empire, numerous foreign conquerors controlled parts of Italy. The Catholic Church and people from other parts of Europe, northern Africa, and Arabic lands all gained control of parts of the Italian peninsula.

Italy was divided between the kingdom of the south and a number of city-states in the north. In the ninth century, Muslims from northern Africa occupied the island of Sicily and established a thriving regime in southern Italy where the arts and education flourished for two centuries. In 1060, invaders from Normandy, a region in southern France, conquered the Muslim region and established themselves in southern Italy. Meanwhile, in northern Italy, villages nestled

More than 200 popes have been Italian, including every pope from 1523 to 1978.

A Byzantine mosaic of Jesus Christ, located in Cefalú, Sicily. The Byzantines left a mark on Italian art and architecture.

POLITICS IN VENICE

Among the Italian city-states, Venice was unique in establishing an early form of constitutional government, an oligarchic constitution, in which the power rests with a small group. As in ancient Rome, the Senate had power, as did another governmental body, the Great Council. The leader of the Senate, the Doge, was elected for life and held a position of great honor.

among the mountainous terrain began establishing independent cultures and identities. By the tenth and eleventh centuries, some of these had merged and expanded to form strong, sovereign city-states.

By the sixteenth century, the most powerful of the Italian city-states had grown to have significant political and economic power in the region. Primary among these city-states were Milan, Venice, Florence, Rome, and Naples. Some city-states were ruled by communes, or town councils, and others were ruled by dynasties of powerful families, such as the Medici family, which dominated politics in Florence for decades. The popes also controlled vast lands, known as the Papal States, which included the city of Rome.

A UNITED ITALY

The Italian city-states were strong and independent, but because they were not united, they were vulnerable to larger nations. In 1494, French forces entered Italy, but they retreated before taking total control. From the 1500s through the 1700s, Spain and Austria also entered the conflict, at times gaining control of Italian lands.

In 1848, a tumultuous year in which revolutions broke out in many European cities, the Italian city-states continued struggling for independence from outside forces. At this point, Austria controlled much of Italy. The kingdom on the island of Sardinia, although under Austrian control, maintained its own constitution. Recognizing that unity would be necessary for independence, Italian patriots worked together to remove the Austrians and unify under the Kingdom of Sardinia.

By 1860, most of northern Italy had been joined to the Kingdom of Sardinia. That same year, a popular Italian freedom fighter and hero named Giuseppe Garibaldi entered Sicily with a volunteer army and

A POPULAR REVOLUTIONARY

Italian revolutionary Giuseppe Garibaldi was born on July 4, 1807, in Nice, France, which was then part of the Kingdom of Sardinia. In 1834, Garibaldi participated in a failed revolt against the king of Sardinia and was forced into exile. He went to South America, where he joined a revolt against the government in Brazil and fought for Uruguay against Argentina. During this time, he formed a volunteer army nicknamed the Red Shirts, based on their attire. Garibaldi returned to Italy with the Red Shirts in 1848 to fight against the Austrians but was again exiled. When he returned in 1854, he joined the fight for unification. In 1860, Garibaldi invaded Sicily, claiming it and southern Italy, a move that was influential in establishing the nation of Italy. During the 1860s and 1870s, he was elected to the Italian Parliament several times. He died on June 2, 1882.

Portrait of Giuseppe Garibaldi, 1860

helped the people of that island win their independence. Garibaldi's small army then continued to the mainland to claim most of southern Italy.

A year later, in 1861, the entire peninsula was finally united into one nation: the Kingdom of Italy. After aiding in the fight to reclaim lands throughout the peninsula, the king of Sardinia, Victor Emmanuel II, was named the first king and ruler of the newly unified nation.

In its first four decades, Italy grew as a nation. Literacy and working conditions improved, and the production of goods increased. Despite these improvements, the Italian people remained mostly unhappy with the government. In 1882, Italy joined with Austria-Hungary and Germany to form the Triple Alliance, an agreement between the three countries to aid and defend one another. That agreement lasted until 1915.

TWO WORLD WARS

In 1915, Italy joined World War I on the side of the Allied powers, which included the United Kingdom, France, and later the United States. Chief among Italy's goals in the war was winning back control of those parts of the country still under Austrian control. Italy gained Trentino–Alto Adige and part of Friuli–Venezia Giulia.

Fascism takes it name from the Latin *fasces*, a bundle of sticks symbolizing punishment in ancient Rome.

Not long after the end of the war, a young Socialist named Benito Mussolini formed a new fascist political party in Italy in

1919. Fascism is a form of government that puts the nation before the individual and tends to place power in the hands of one ruler or dictator.

As Mussolini's popular appeal and political power grew, so did his ambitions. In 1922, Mussolini and his followers marched into Rome and demanded that they be given control of the government. Confronted with the power of the movement, King Victor Emmanuel III put Mussolini in charge. This change in leadership resulted in more than two decades of fascist dictatorship in Italy. Those years were marked by unlimited executive authority, a severely restrictive society, and violations of human rights. Mussolini aimed to capture Ethiopia and then entered World War II on the side of Nazi Germany in 1940.

In 1943, Victor Emmanuel III mandated that Mussolini be removed from power and surrendered the nation to the Allied powers. Mussolini was rescued by German forces and went to northern Italy. Germany then tried to take control of Italy, establishing Mussolini as the head of a puppet government the Germans would control. Joined by a number of Resistance forces (Italians against fascism and Nazism), the Allies reclaimed Italy. In 1945, Mussolini was shot and killed by the Resistance as he tried to escape Italy.

Between 1945 and 1994, the Italian government changed leaders on average every 11 months.

Not long after the end of Mussolini's dictatorship, in 1946, the Italian people voted to end the monarchy. Only briefly on the throne, King Umberto II left the country, and the modern republic of Italy was formed. Since that time, Italy has remained a unified and independent nation with a republican,

Benito Mussolini, *left*, with Adolf Hitler, 1938

Italy has struggled with political disunity since World War II.

or parliamentary, government. Even so, the nation's origin as a group of powerful, independent entities has remained a strong influence.

GROWTH AND CHANGE

The second half of the twentieth century was a time of tremendous growth and change for Italy. Guided by members of the Allied powers from the United States and the United Kingdom, the Italians drafted a new constitution and instituted a democratic government. But regional affiliations and identities remained powerful, and it was unclear how wholeheartedly the nation embraced unification.

Over the past 65 years, the young democracy has struggled with a weak centralized government that has been marked by corruption and division. Italy's numerous political parties have included those with Socialist, Communist, and anarchist platforms. In addition, the nation has endured attacks and threats from homegrown political terrorists and organized crime families.

Despite these challenges, Italy quickly developed a vibrant new economy based on its numerous family-owned businesses, many with a strong sense of craftsmanship and style. Today, Italian fashion houses, car manufacturers, and design companies are recognized as some of the best in the world. However, Italy struggles to compete in the global marketplace and faces a number of economic challenges in the twenty-first century.

CHAPTER 5

PEOPLE: GRACE AND STYLE

Italy encompasses communities ranging from cosmopolitan cities to small farming and fishing villages. Within each region of the nation, the people enjoy distinctive food and traditions. Yet Italians also share a rich artistic heritage, a lengthy historical legacy, a strong belief in the importance of family, and a distinctive culture and language.

The official language of Italy is Italian, and it is spoken throughout most of the country. Italian is characterized as a Romance language, similar to French and Spanish, which means that it is derived from Latin. People in different regions of Italy speak distinct dialects, but the standard form of Italian is widely spoken and is used in schools and on television. This comes from the dialect of Tuscany. Differences in dialects include the pronunciations of certain words and phrases.

Dining together is an important way Italians connect with family and friends.

ITALIAN GERMAN CULTURE

The mild climate and strategic location of the Trentino–Alto Adige region in northern Italy, a major passing point through the Alps, has been attractive to numerous conquerors over the years. Previously part of Austria, the region was granted to Italy after World War I. As a result, it has experienced ethnic tensions between German and Italian residents.

Trentino–Alto Adige has a mixed Italian and German culture. The northern part has a distinctly German influence in architecture and cuisine, and many residents still speak German. But the southern part is more Mediterranean in character, and most residents speak Italian.

A few communities in Italy speak languages other than Italian. For example, some groups in the north, in the Trentino–Alto Adige, speak German. There is also a French-speaking community in Valle d'Aosta and a Slovene-speaking area of Friuli–Venezia Giulia.

THE ITALIAN PEOPLE

In July 2011, Italy had an estimated population of 61,016,804.[1] The vast majority of Italians are of Italian ethnicity. However, there are smaller communities of Italians of mixed ethnicity, including German Italians, French Italians, and Slovene Italians in the north and Albanian Italians and Greek Italians in the south.

At one time, Italy consisted primarily of small villages and towns, where the inhabitants struggled to farm the rough and mountainous land.

Over the years, as the population has shifted into cities, fewer people have worked the land. Since the 1950s, Italians have been moving from small villages to urban areas. This has led to an increase in the urban population, which comprised 68 percent of Italians in 2010.[2] The country's three largest cities—Rome, Milan, and Naples—have a combined population of more than 8 million people.[3] Large metropolitan neighborhoods surround these cities.

The majority of Italians, 65.9 percent, are between 15 and 64 years of age. An estimated 20.3 percent are aged

YOU SAY IT!

English	Italian
Hello	Ciao (CHOW)
Good-bye	Arrivederci (ah-ree-vah-DARE-chee)
Good morning / Good afternoon	Buon giorno (bwohn-JOHR-noh)
Good evening	Buona sera (bwoh-nah say-rah)
Thank you	Grazie (grah-tsee-ay)
You're welcome	Prego (pray-goh)

65 or older, and only 13.8 percent of Italians are between the ages of zero and 14.[4] In fact, Italy has one of the lowest birthrates in the world, with an average of 1.39 children per every Italian woman.[5]

Italy has the tenth-highest average life expectancy in the world, at 81.77 years.[6] However, Italian women live on average six years longer than men. Women live to an average age of 84.53 and men to 79.16.[7]

FAMILY AND RELIGION

The history and culture of Italy are in many ways tied to the Roman Catholic Church. The Italian government is secular, and only 15 percent of Italians attend church regularly, according to a 2007 study. Regardless, 90 percent of Italians are believed to be Roman Catholic. The remaining 10 percent are Jewish or Protestant, and a newly growing Muslim population is composed mostly of recent immigrants to Italy.[8]

The Catholic Church has also influenced the culture and society through religious holidays and social customs, although it does not set the country's laws. For example, in 1970, the Italian people voted to allow divorce, despite the church's laws against it. More recently, the Catholic Church has called for Italian women to return to their traditional roles as wives and mothers in response to the nation's continually declining birthrate. The church's request has largely been ignored, however, as Italian women make up approximately half of the total workforce.

**Centuries ago, this Sicilian cathedral was a mosque.
Italy's Muslim population today is growing.**

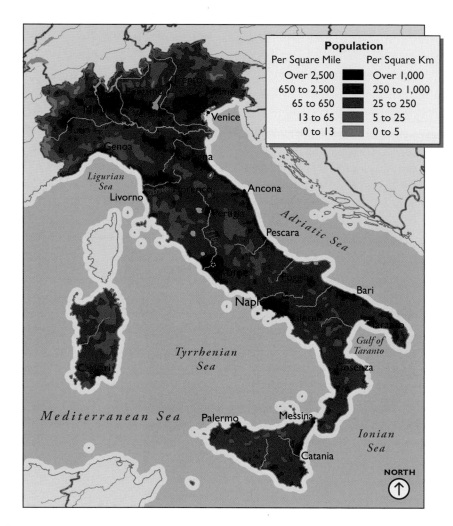

Population Density of Italy

Many of the social changes in Italy have been led by women, who have, since the 1970s, consistently pushed for increased gender equality in work and in legislation. Their efforts have resulted In providing maternity leave from work and establishing more nurseries. But despite these gains, women remain the primary caregivers in families.

Social and family ties are important to Italians. For centuries, extended families lived together, and grandparents regularly cared for grandchildren while the parents worked. In Italy, adults traditionally remain with their families until shortly before marriage. Approximately 60 percent of Italians between the ages of 18 and 34 live with their parents.[9] But more and more contemporary Italians are living in nuclear families. Young, single adults are moving out more often than those of previous generations, although both families and single adults tend to reside near their parents.

The relationship between a mother and her son has special prominence in Italy. In fact, it has earned the nickname *mammismo,* roughly translated as "mommyism," which indicates the closeness between a mother and her son.

MOVING OUT

More young adult Italians are choosing to live on their own before marriage, and women are moving out more often than men. In 2006, one study reported that by age 29, half of Italian men still lived at their parents' homes, compared to only one-quarter of Italian women.[10] Eight out of ten Italian men between the ages of 18 and 30 lived with their parents.[11]

Family is also important to jobs and occupations in Italy. Family and community connections help Italians get jobs and meet the people who can help them succeed. For example, a young man's uncle or aunt might introduce him to the company that will hire him for his first job, or a teen girl's cousins might help her meet the head of an exclusive private school, making admission more likely. Similarly, having a friend's recommendation might assist one in gaining a lucrative business contract.

In addition, a majority of Italian companies, including some of the largest and most successful, are family owned. Examples include the car company Fiat and the tire company Pirelli.

Italy has the tenth-lowest infant mortality rate in the world.

Many Italian mothers and sons have a uniquely close bond.

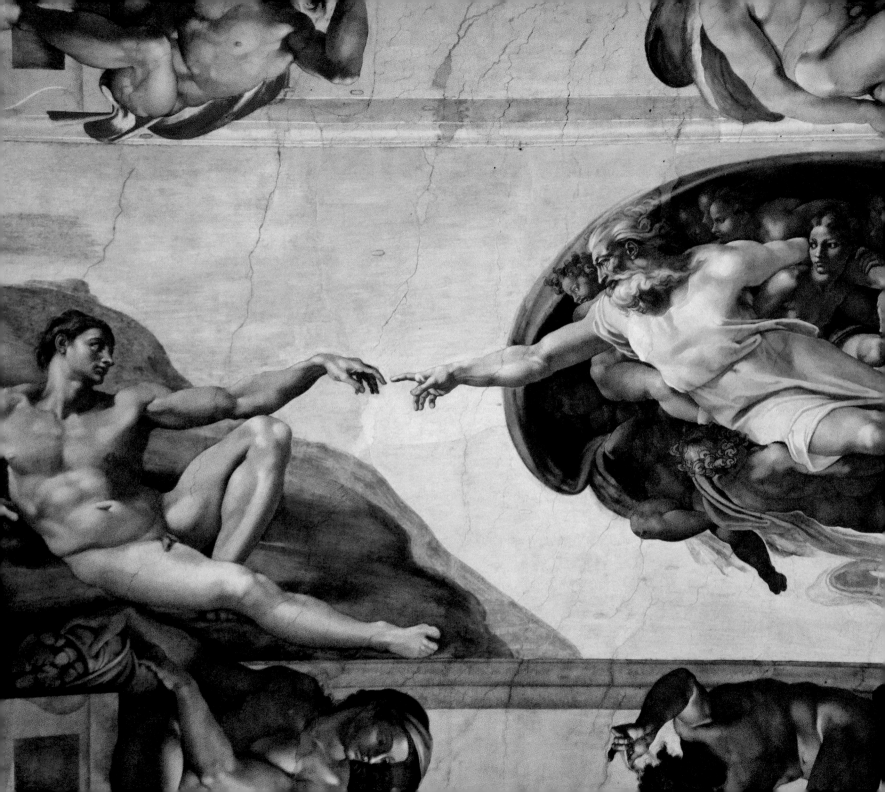

CHAPTER 6
CULTURE:
ART AND BEAUTY

Italy enjoys a lively and artistic culture with a cuisine that is famous throughout the world. Much of the history of Western art is tied to the innovations of Italian artists and musicians. Italy is the birthplace of opera, the home of Renaissance painting, and one of the fashion capitals of the world.

Design and attention to detail are important to Italians. The common expression *la bella figura,* meaning "the beautiful figure," inspires Italians to look their best. That idea comes across not only in the Italian style of dress but also in the approach to daily life and in the creative talents of Italy's internationally famous designers, architects, artists, musicians, and filmmakers.

Michelangelo (1475–1564) was a renowned painter, sculptor, and architect.

Michelangelo's *Creation of Adam* in the Sistine Chapel in Rome

FESTIVALS

Throughout the year, Italians share their enjoyment of food and beauty through *feste*, or "festivals." There are three main types of festivals: religious festivals based on saints' days and other celebrations of the Roman Catholic Church, civic or secular festivals, and a form of festivals called *sagre*, which revolve around agriculture or nature.

Primary church holidays, such as Christmas and Easter, are important throughout Italy. Among the *sagre* are a number of festivals to celebrate particular crops, such as the autumn harvest of grapes and olives celebrated in central Italy.

The Italian calendar is filled with numerous *feste* throughout the year. The culture's artistic influence is evident in the celebration of

CARNEVALE

Italians observe Lent, the season before Easter, with fasting and sacrifice. In preparation for this time of austerity, the nation enjoys one of its most fascinating and dramatic festivals, Carnevale, or Carnival. As winter turns to spring, Italians celebrate with rich feasts, masked balls, parades, and special foods, including sausages and *frittelle*, or fried sweets filled with fruit or cream and dusted with sugar. Carnevale's main event is a weeklong celebration culminating in Martedì Grasso, or Mardi Gras, which is also called Fat Tuesday.

Although Carnevale celebrations vary from region to region, one of the most famous occurs in Venice. Venetian revelry goes back to the twelfth century and has included tightrope walking, bullfighting, and, most notably, masked balls. Venetian masks are elegant and stylized, and over the years, mask making has developed into a specialized craft.

public festivals, which often involve elaborate costumes, masks, banners, and other forms of regalia.

A HAVEN FOR FOOD LOVERS

Italian cuisine is popular in many areas of the world. Pasta and pizza, in particular, have been perfected by the Italians over the centuries. In fact, what passes for Italian food in other countries is not usually acceptable in Italy. In 2008, the Italian Academy of Cuisine announced that, on average, six out of ten Italian dishes prepared in Italian restaurants outside Italy were made incorrectly.[1]

Two key concepts are at the heart of Italian cuisine. First, the most important aspect of authentic Italian cooking is the selection of fresh ingredients. Ingredients are carefully chosen to balance flavors, colors, and textures. Second, food is integral to Italian culture. Meals are enjoyed slowly and provide a time to socialize and relax. Lunch—a relaxed period of time also called

THE SLOW FOOD MOVEMENT

When US fast-food company McDonald's opened a restaurant in Rome, Carlo Petrini founded the Slow Food movement in protest. The movement is dedicated to preserving traditional foods and biodiversity in agriculture. What Petrini began as a small association in Barolo, a town in the wine-growing region of Piedmont, soon spread to Paris and beyond. Today, the movement has more than 100,000 members in 100 countries. As Petrini has stated, everyone should "slowly, fully and without excess enjoy the pleasures of the senses."[2]

A focus on fresh, gourmet ingredients distinguishes authentic Italian food.

la pausa, or "the pause"—can last up to two or three hours and include multiple courses. Italy's emphasis on cooking with fresh, locally grown ingredients and taking the time to enjoy meals inspired what has become an international movement called Slow Food.

The staple of Italian food is pasta. Evidence suggests Arabs brought pasta to Italy by the early Middle Ages. Pasta comes in a variety of shapes and sizes. It is often prepared with a tomato-based sauce, but sauces can be made from cream or herbs, as well.

Italian meals are typically served in multiple courses. The meal begins with antipasti, or appetizers, such as bread with olive oil and vinegar for dipping and olives. Other antipasti options are *grissini*, bread sticks from Turin; bruschetta, toasted bread with a fresh topping such as tomatoes or an olive spread; or *insalata caprese*, mozzarella cheese with tomatoes and basil. The first course, or *primo*, generally consists of pasta or risotto, a creamy rice dish. A wide variety of pasta specialties include vegetarian or meat-based options such as *pasta con pesto*, with basil paste; *risotto alla Milanese*, saffron risotto with veal; and *spaghetti con le vongole,* spaghetti with clam sauce. Some meals end after the *primo*, but for a longer and luxurious meal, a second course, or *secondi*, consists of meat, fish, or a side dish such as cooked vegetables. Finally come *frutti e dolci*, fruit and sweets, which are followed by coffee, a hearty and steaming hot espresso.

Ivrea commemorates the beginning of Lent with a village-wide food fight, the Battle of the Oranges.

Not all meals are quite so involved. Italian breakfasts feature the same hot espresso, but it is normally served with a pastry such as a *cornetto*, a buttery, sweet bread, or *crostata*, a flaky fruit-filled pastry. Dinners are less elaborate than lunches but tend to feature pasta and can be as lengthy and layered as lunches, depending on the occasion.

Italy is famous for its wines, and wine is a regular part of most meals. Grappa, an alcoholic beverage made from the grape seeds and stalks discarded when making wine, is a distinctly Italian drink made since the Middle Ages. It is popular after meals.

SPORTS AND GAMES

Italians enjoy many sports, including cycling, auto racing, and soccer. Sports enthusiasts earn the nickname *tifosi*, or "feverish fans." During the first half of the twentieth century, cycling was one of Italy's most popular sports, and the nation boasted world-class cyclists. For example, in 1909, Luigi Ganna won

FAUSTO COPPI

In 1949 and again in 1952, Italian cyclist Fausto Coppi won the sport's biggest race, the Tour de France. In the same years, he also won the Giro d'Italia, the first cyclist to win the world's top two races in the same year. In 1953, Coppi won two more major races: the Giro d'Italia once again and the World Championship Road Race.

Bicyclists race through Perugia, 2011.

the first ever Giro d'Italia, an important cycling competition. Later, Alfredo Binda became the five-time winner of the Giro d'Italia, and he won the World Championship Road Race three times—in 1927, 1930, and 1932—which remains a world record.[3] Two decades later, Italy had another world-champion cyclist in Fausto Coppi.

Today, the most popular sport among Italians is soccer, known as *calico*, or football. Italians play the game in sports clubs across the country. Italian soccer players are considered some of the best in the world, including goalie Gianluigi Buffon and defender Fabio Cannavaro, who was captain of the Italian team when it won the World Cup in 2006 and 2010. Soccer can ignite old rivalries between cities, and fans travel the country to cheer on their favorite teams. Some of the most popular teams include Juventus from Turin, Lazio from Rome, and AC Milan.

Taking advantage of the country's long seacoast, water sports are also common, including diving, swimming, and water polo. Snow skiing is a popular winter sport in the mountains.

ART AND ARCHITECTURE

From the ancient Roman Colosseum to the ceiling of the Sistine Chapel, from Michelangelo's marble statue *David* to da Vinci's painting *The Last Supper*, Italy is home to some of the most famous art and architecture in the history of the world.

Influential Italian architecture dates back to ancient Rome. The fact that some of the Romans' architectural feats, such as the Pantheon and the Colosseum, are still standing attests to their excellent construction methods. The Romans designed improved roads, plumbing, and aqueducts. Roman engineering and architectural inventions changed how cities looked and were constructed.

Italy's roster of native artists includes such masters as Leonardo da Vinci, Michelangelo, Raphael, Donatello, and Botticelli. These and other artists, many from Italy, were responsible for the primary innovations in Western art during a time known as the Renaissance in the fifteenth and sixteenth centuries. Notable among these are naturalistic and realistic painting and the discovery of perspective, or how to depict objects as if they are receding into the distance.

The person responsible for discovering the mathematical formula that allowed painters to use perspective was architect Filippo Brunelleschi. He designed the dome of one of Italy's most famous

ROMAN ENGINEERS

Rome's Cloaca Maxima, or "Big Sewer," was built and improved between the sixth and third centuries BCE. It was the first of its kind in the world, and amazingly, it is still in use today. Roman engineers built aqueducts, creating a clean water supply for the city. This led to flushable toilets, public and private baths, steam rooms, and water fountains. The Romans also designed a complex network of roads and, consequently, a postal system, allowing messages to be transported with ease around the vast empire.

Il Duomo in Florence

cathedrals, Il Duomo, or "The Dome," in Florence. In 1418, Brunelleschi won a contest to make the dome for the cathedral. The egg-shaped dome, the first of its kind, was erected without scaffolding.

This relationship between art and architecture typifies the Renaissance, a time when connections between various fields were emphasized. Many of the most accomplished artists were also influential in other areas. A prime example is Leonardo da Vinci, an accomplished artist, inventor, scientist, and mathematician. His peers, including the renowned sculptor Michelangelo and the influential painter Raphael, were also skilled architects. Other influential Italian artists include Titian, Caravaggio, and Tintoretto.

Some of Italy's many notable buildings include cathedrals in the Byzantine, Gothic, and Baroque styles. Commissioned by the Roman Catholic Church, these cathedrals reflect the

REVIVING ANTIQUITY

The Renaissance began in Italy in the 1300s and spread throughout Europe until approximately 1600. The word *Renaissance* derives from the Latin word for "rebirth," which is *renascor*. Scholars and artists of the Renaissance studied the arts and learning of ancient Greece and Rome, engaging in a renewal or rebirth of these ancient ideas. Given this, the Renaissance is sometimes referred to as the "Revival of Antiquity." It came after a period of history known as the Middle Ages, in which theology, or the study of God, was primary. In contrast, Renaissance scholars put humanity at the center of intellectual pursuits, studying the accomplishments of cultures throughout time and history and inventing a new field: the humanities.

GALILEO GALILEI

One of the greatest scientists in history, Galileo Galilei, made numerous contributions to astronomy and physics in the sixteenth century. Born February 15, 1564, in Pisa, Galileo showed talent in mathematics from a young age. In 1609, he built his first telescope and used it to make a number of discoveries, including the moons of Jupiter. Galileo made many more important discoveries throughout his life—most notably, the law of the pendulum and the law of freely falling bodies, which states that objects fall at the same speed regardless of their mass.

Galileo's writings in support of a theory by Polish astronomer Nicolaus Copernicus—stating that planets revolve around the sun, not Earth—put him in opposition with the Catholic Church. A lifelong, devout Catholic, Galileo was imprisoned by the church for his scientific writings, specifically those about the Copernican theory. He died in isolation on January 8, 1642. Centuries later, the church recanted, and in 1992, Pope John Paul II publicly endorsed a church commission that concluded Galileo should not have been condemned.

work of many architects and artists. But churches are not the only marvels of Italian architecture.

As the birthplace of opera, Italy is home to one of the world's most famous opera houses, the Teatro alla Scala, or "Theatre at the Stairway." Originally constructed by the empress of Austria in 1778, the building was repaired after being bombed during World War II. The elaborate interior of La Scala, as the theater is known, has five tiers of boxes for seating.

Italy has nurtured other artistic crafts as well. Carrara is considered the world's capital for marble sculpture. Venice—specifically, the island of Murano—was an international center for glassmaking for centuries.

Although Italians did not continue to lead the arts in the twentieth century, Italy was home to at least two important Modernist movements. The first, called futurism, was an avant-garde movement that Italian artist Filippo Marinetti initiated in 1909 and lasted through World War I. The second, arte povera, or "poor art," which used everyday materials such as soil, cement, and newspapers, originated in Italy in 1967 and lasted through the 1970s. In addition to Marinetti, famous Italian artists of the twentieth century include Giorgio de Chirico, Carlo Carrá, and Alberto Burri.

In contemporary times, Italian architect Renzo Piano is internationally renowned. Piano designed the Auditorium Parco della Musica in Rome in 2002 and has been commissioned to create museums and buildings in the United States and Europe.

MUSIC AND THEATER

Perhaps the largest contribution Italy made to musical history was the invention of opera in Florence in 1600. Incredibly popular in Italy and widely appreciated the world over, opera is an art form that tells dramatic and passionate tales through a specialized type of singing. Famous Italian opera composers from the nineteenth and early twentieth centuries include Gioachino Rossini, Giuseppe Verdi, and Giacomo Puccini.

Talented Italian tenor Luciano Pavarotti increased opera's popularity worldwide.

Notable classical musicians include Antonio Vivaldi and Luciano Pavarotti. Vivaldi, composer of *The Four Seasons* and other classical pieces, lived in Venice during the eighteenth century at a time when the city was renowned for its musical conservatories. Pavarotti was an immensely popular opera singer in the twentieth century.

Italian musical history does not end with figures from the past. Contemporary Italian music known as *musica leggera*, or "light music," has become popular. This category spans rock, jazz, folk, hip-hop, and pop. Punk rock is celebrated at an annual music festival, Rock in Idro, in Milan.

Italians' theatrical impulse, so evident in opera, comes out in the nation's varied forms of theater and a history of comic theater. In Sicily, large, painted marionettes act out tales of chivalry and gallantry with humor and spirit. And *Commedia dell'arte*—a form of comic theater that began in Italy in the sixteenth century and is believed to derive from ancient Roman culture—features playful characters in slapstick and bawdy storylines.

LITERATURE AND FILM

From ancient poets to contemporary novelists, Italy has an expansive and impressive history of literature. Two among the many giants of ancient literature are Roman poets Virgil and Ovid, authors of *Aeneid* and *Metamorphoses*, respectively. Thirteenth-century writer Dante Alighieri, author of *The Divine Comedy*, described the layers of hell in a book that continues to fascinate readers and scholars. In 1906, poet Giosuè Carducci became the first Italian to win the Nobel Prize in Literature.

The modern piano was invented in Florence in 1709.

Italian writers have long drawn on the country's complex and often troubled past. Primo Levi, an Italian Jewish scientist and author, was detained in Auschwitz, one of the notorious death camps of World War II. His autobiographical account of the experience, *If This Is a Man*, was published in 1947. Grazia Deledda won the Nobel Prize in Literature in 1926 for her fictionalized memoir about the trials of growing up in rural Sardinia. Among other notable Italian authors are Umberto Eco, best-selling author of *The Name of the Rose*, poet and Nobel laureate Eugenio Montale, and imaginative novelist Italo Calvino.

The most influential Italian filmmakers include Luchino Visconti, Bernardo Bertolucci, and Michelangelo Antonioni. Perhaps most famous of all is Federico Fellini, widely considered one of the best filmmakers of all time. Famous Italian actors include Sophia Loren, voted most popular female star in the world in 1969, and Marcello Mastroianni, winner of several best actor awards at the Cannes Film Festival and other competitions.

DESIGN FOR EVERYDAY

Italian design company Alessi is a family-owned operation with an emphasis on style and craftsmanship. Based on Lake Orta in the Italian Alps, the company has been making whimsical products for daily use in the home since 1935. But rather than rely on the skills of one owner or designer, Alessi employs a number of freelance designers in a tradition known as the Italian Design Factory: a system in which a small- to medium-sized company specializes in one area, similar to traditional workshops from the Renaissance. Alessi designers have an eye for fusing art, design, and purpose in everyday items, ranging from teakettles to trash cans.

Federico Fellini on set, 1972

FASHION AND DESIGN

Italy's emphasis on style, design, and artistry has led to economic, commercial, and artistic success in the fields of fashion and design. As is typical of Italian businesses, even many of those that have achieved world-class fame are family owned. Their success has been fueled by a mixture of passion, dedication, and creativity.

Renowned Italian fashion designers include Valentino, Armani, and some of the world's most famous and luxurious fashion houses: Gucci, Fendi, Ferragamo, Prada, and Missoni. Italian design also inspires four of the sleekest and most sought after brands of sports cars: Maserati, Fiat, Ferrari, and Lamborghini.

Armani collection on the runway in Milan's Fashion Week, 2006

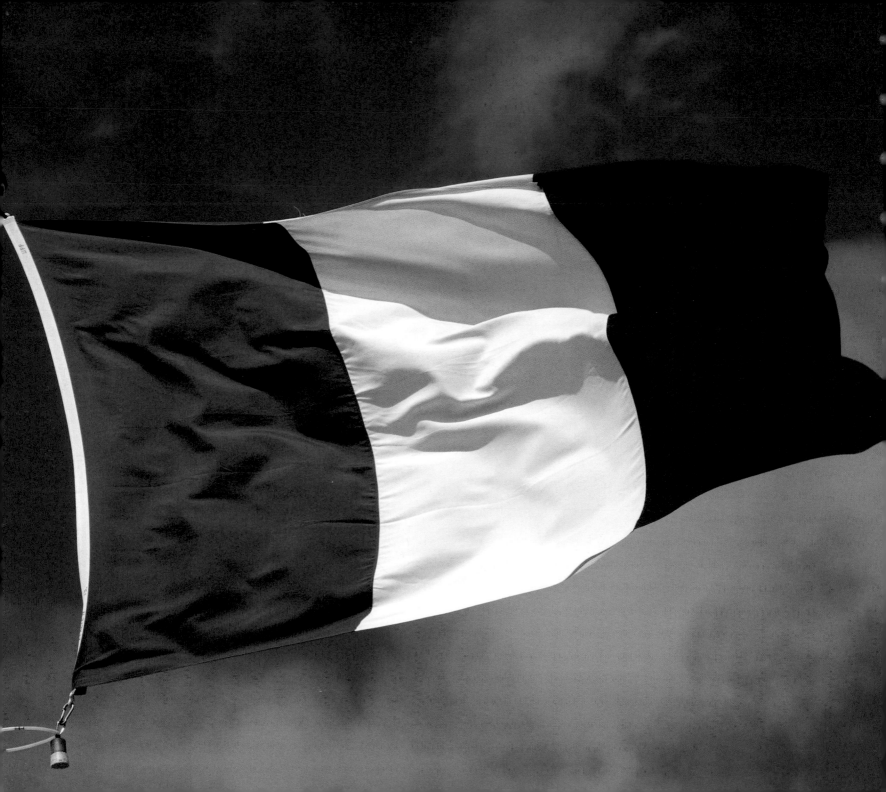

CHAPTER 7
POLITICS: MANY VOICES

In 1957, Italy joined with France, Germany, and other European nations to found an economic and political partnership. That partnership was outlined in the Treaty of Rome and went into effect on January 1, 1958. It established the European Economic Community, which has come to be called simply the European Union, or EU for short.

Flag of Italy

THE FLAG OF ITALY

The Italian flag is divided vertically into thirds: green, white, and red. The colors have been used to represent Italy since the eighteenth century. Some evidence suggests the colors were based on the uniforms of Milan's city militia. Sardinian revolutionaries adopted the colors in 1848, and it became the national flag when Italy united in 1870.

THE EUROPEAN UNION

The EU was founded in an effort to provide "peace, prosperity and freedom for its 498 million citizens—in a fairer, safer world."[2] Some of the EU's accomplishments thus far have included easy travel and trade between EU nations; establishment of a single European currency, the euro; joint action against crime and terrorism; and an improved standard of living in some poor regions of Europe.

Italy was a founding member of the EU, which today consists of 27 independent nations united by common interests.[1] And Italy continues to thrive as a nation within the body of the EU.

Italy is officially called the Repubblica Italiana, or Italian Republic. Since 1948, the Italian government has experienced frequent changes of power. These changes, along with charges of corruption leveled at various government officials over time, seem to have led the Italian people to distrust their centralized government.

Many Italians put more trust in family and community loyalties. Some argue that the importance of family ties has led to a weaker government, but others see the emphasis on family allegiances as a result of what they perceive as unsteady leadership of the country since unification. In addition, illegal immigration, organized crime, and unequal distribution of wealth from the north to the south pose persistent challenges in Italy.

The Italian Parliament meets at Montecitorio in Rome.

STRUCTURE OF THE GOVERNMENT OF ITALY

Executive	Legislative	Judicial
President Prime minister Council of Ministers	Senato della Repubblica (Senate) Camera dei Deputati (Chamber of Deputies)	Corte Costituzionale (Constitutional Court) Supreme Court of Cassation lower courts

THE ITALIAN GOVERNMENT

When Italy unified on March 17, 1861, as the Kingdom of Italy, it was governed by a monarchy supported by a parliament. This changed in the 1920s, when Benito Mussolini established a fascist dictatorship in Italy. Not long after Mussolini was ousted and the kingdom restored, the people voted for another change, ending the monarchy and initiating the contemporary republic.

Today, Italy is a republic, which means the Italian people elect officials to represent them. The government consists of three branches: an executive branch, a legislative branch, and a judicial branch.

Italy's executive branch includes the president, the prime minister, and the Council of Ministers. The president is the chief of state and the chief of the armed forces. He or she is elected to a seven-year term by Parliament and 58 regional representatives. Italy does not have a vice president, so if the president becomes ill or dies, the president of the Senate assumes the nation's presidency. Italy's prime minister is the head of the government and the president of the Council of Ministers, or cabinet, which is a body of advisers. The prime minister is appointed by the president, most often from among members of Parliament. In determining national policy, the Italian prime minister plays the most important role.

Italy's legislative branch is composed of the Parlamento, or Parliament. It is divided into two houses: the 315-member Senato della Repubblica, or Senate, and the 630-member Camera dei Deputati, or Chamber of Deputies. Members of both houses are elected by the Italian people and serve five-year terms. Members of the Senate are elected by proportional vote, meaning that seats are assigned to political parties based on the percentages of people in them. Up to five members are also appointed for life by the president. Members of the Chamber of Deputies are elected by popular vote.

The judicial branch of the Italian government is headed by the Corte Costituzionale, or Constitutional Court. One-third of the 15 judges are appointed by the president, one-third are elected by Parliament, and one-third are elected by the lower courts. The Constitutional Court has the power to determine if laws are constitutional, and it resolves conflicts among the regions or the branches of the central government. Italy also has a system of lower courts, the highest of which is the Supreme Court of Cassation. These lower courts are part of one national system; the regions do not have their own separate court systems.

The Italian constitution was passed on December 11, 1947, and went into effect on January 1, 1948. To help create a more equitable judicial system, the new constitution provided new levels of protection for federal judges and prosecutors.

Italians over the age of 18 may vote in all elections except for the Senate. To vote in this election, they must be at least 25 years old.

A LEGACY OF INFLUENCE

Italy's political history is long and complex and has been marked by a number of influential politicians and thinkers. The legacies of the Roman Senate and various Roman emperors, such as Augustus and Julius Caesar, continue to be studied in political science, law, and history courses today.

Over time, areas of Italy were ruled by different nations. For many decades, a theocracy headed by the Roman Catholic Church controlled large portions of the peninsula. The popes still govern in the Vatican, which remains a sovereign nation within the boundaries of Rome.

For nearly two centuries, Italy was a nation of strong city-states, each governed independently. During this era, politician and philosopher Niccolò Machiavelli wrote the celebrated but controversial *The Prince* in 1513, and criminologist and economist Cesare Beccaria wrote *On Crimes and Punishments* in 1764. Both books are highly regarded for drawing connections between politics and law and humanistic ideals, which value human dignity, intelligence, and contributions to society. These writings continue to influence the way governments are organized and laws are made and passed.

CURRENT LEADERS

In 2011, Italy's executive branch consisted of President Giorgio Napolitano, who has been in office since May 15, 2006, and Prime Minister Silvio Berlusconi, who began his third term of office on May 8, 2008. Berlusconi had been in office eight of the first ten years of the

A CONTROVERSIAL AND COLORFUL LEADER

Silvio Berlusconi was born in Milan on September 29, 1936. As a young man, he sold vacuum cleaners and worked as a singer on cruise ships. He completed a law degree in 1961 and soon after set up a construction firm called Edilnord. He established himself as a successful developer, building a series of new residential housing facilities in and around the city of Milan.

Berlusconi followed this entrepreneurial success by founding a cable TV company, which soon grew into the nation's biggest media corporation. He also acquired Italy's largest newspaper and publishing firm, making him a publishing magnate and one of the richest and most powerful men in Italy. Another of Berlusconi's purchases was the popular soccer team AC Milan. When he entered politics in 1993, he founded his own political party and called it Forza Italia, or Go Italy. He based the party name on a chant used by soccer fans.

Berlusconi was appointed prime minister for the first time in 1994 but left the office after being accused of tax fraud. He returned to the office in 2001 and remained prime minister until 2006. He was appointed again in 2008 and remained in office despite calls that he step down due to ongoing personal scandal.

Prime Minister Silvio Berlusconi, *left*, and President Giorgio Napolitano in 2011

twentieth century, making him the longest-serving Italian prime minister since World War II.

Berlusconi is also one of the nation's wealthiest citizens and has been the subject of criticism and gossip. In 2001, Berlusconi pledged to run the country like a corporation. However, the nation was soon plagued by economic challenges. In recent years, the prime minister has been embroiled in personal scandals. In 2009, he endured a very public divorce initiated by his wife, former actress Veronica Lario, which included allegations of infidelity. Lario's charges that Berlusconi flirted with young women were embarrassing, but other allegations, made in 2011, were more damaging. Most controversial are charges that the prime minister employed an underage prostitute and held wildly elaborate state parties—both charges he has rejected.

POLITICAL PARTIES

The many and diverse interests present in Italy are expressed in its political parties. Through much of the latter part of the twentieth century, a conservative party called the Partito della Democrazia Cristiana (DC), or Christian Democrats, dominated Italian politics. For many years, the Partito Comunista Italiano (PCI), or Italian Communist Party—the largest Communist party in Europe—was the second most important party in Italy. From after World War II until the 1970s, the PCI remained influential, even though it was barred from government. The PCI's popularity began declining in the 1980s and continued until it split into two parties in 1991: the Democrats of the Left Party and the Partito della Rifondazione Comunista, or the Communist Refoundation Party.

Italian women received partial voting rights in 1925 and full suffrage in 1945.

TERRORISM IN ITALY

Radical political parties in Italy have been responsible for terrorist acts in the past. A militant offshoot of the Communist Party, the Red Brigade, was responsible for bombings and political assassinations, including the kidnap and murder of former Italian prime minister Aldo Moro in 1978. The Red Brigade and another neofascist group both claimed responsibility for the 1980 bombing of Bologna, which killed at least 75 people.[3] As recently as 2010, the anarchist group Federazione Anarchica Informale, or the Informal Anarchist Federation, claimed responsibility for numerous bombings of diplomatic embassies around Italy.

In 2001, the moderate conservative Forza Italia party, the party of Prime Minister Berlusconi, took the majority of votes and led the government. Other parties with conservative leanings are the Lega Norda (LN) and Movement for Autonomy (MpA). In 2007, two of the more central-leaning liberal groups merged to form the Democratic Party (PD). Other current but smaller political parties in Italy include the liberal Italy of Values (IdV), the Future and Liberty Party (FLI), and the Union of the Center (UdC).

The Italian Socialist Party, which has taken different formations and names over the years, has also been popular with a small but consistent group of Italians. Another group that has remained in Italy since at least the early twentieth century is the anarchist party, an unofficial affiliation of people who are against organized government. The popularity of leftist and radical groups, particularly among youth in the universities, led to unrest and fears of terrorism.

SPECIAL INTERESTS

Italian politics is marked by a diversity of points of view and has long suffered from what is called clientelism, or the exchange of special favors. Steady, high-paying jobs in government and bureaucracy are often assigned to people based on their political, familial, religious, or economic associations, not their qualifications to do the work. Although not all Italian politicians are corrupt, many take advantage of the government's lack of control over trading influence or jobs for votes and practicing other forms of corruption.

The Roman Catholic Church, centered in the Vatican, has long been a powerful force in Italy, and historically, it has influenced both government and society. For example, just prior to World War II, Mussolini made numerous concessions to Catholicism so that the church would accept the fascist state. The most famous of these, the Lateran Treaty, resulted in the formation of the Vatican as a tiny, independent nation in 1929. More recently, the church has had less influence, particularly in relation to social values and customs. Despite the fact that the Catholic Church has always opposed divorce and birth control, the Italian people voted to legalize both in the 1970s.

Benedict XVI became pope in 2005.

The government has also struggled against the powerful reach of organized crime syndicates, which date back to the nineteenth century. These include the Camorra family, which is primarily active in Naples,

and the Mafia, based on the island of Sicily. Italy's government and police forces have tried for decades to suppress the violence and economic control associated with these groups, particularly in southern Italy. The Italian shopkeepers association, Confesercenti, told Reuters in 2008, "Every day a huge mass of money goes out of the pockets of Italian shopkeepers and entrepreneurs and into those of the mafias, something like 250 million euros a day, 10 million an hour and 160,000 a minute."[4] Some Italian politicians have even bowed to the pressure and made deals with the criminals.

Camorra family boss Cesare Pagano was arrested by Italian police in 2010.

CHAPTER 8
ECONOMICS: THE STRENGTH OF FAMILIES

After World War II, Italy's economy began steady and impressive growth. The era of the 1950s and 1960s has been referred to as an "economic miracle" for Italy, mostly because of the nation's shift from an agricultural to an industrial economy. During this time, Italians' average income increased faster than the incomes of any other Europeans.[1] Whereas In the first half of the twentieth century, Italians generally made just enough money to get by, by midcentury, more and more Italians were able to purchase items such as refrigerators, televisions, and cars.

Industrialization also meant that more Italians moved to urban centers, reshaping the nation's cultural landscape. During the 1950s and 1960s, an estimated 8 to 9 million people moved to the north and to

Families are the pillars of the Italian economy.

cities in Italy.[2] Although the family remained the cornerstone of Italian society, many people left their families and moved to find work. In addition, the number of wage earners in the typical family increased. By the 1970s, women had entered the workforce in large numbers, creating a new trend that helped influence the equal rights legislation of that decade.

Interestingly, Italian family businesses were not split up by industrialization as much as enriched by it. Compared to other countries, Italy's economic growth was mostly fueled by companies that were—and remain—family owned. From the large tire company Pirelli and the successful clothing company Benetton to numerous smaller businesses, including restaurants, stores, and artisan workshops, family-owned companies make up the majority of businesses in Italy.

The Italian GDP dropped by 5.1 percent in 2009.

Italy's economic growth continued through much of the second half of the twentieth century. Similar to many nations, Italy struggled during the worldwide recession that began in 2007. Unemployment rose from 6.8 percent in 2007 to 8.4 percent in 2010. Even so, the overall economy grew by 1 percent in 2010 and the gross domestic product (GDP) was $1.782 trillion, the eleventh largest in the world.[3]

In 2010, the per capita GDP, or the total economic production of the country divided by its population, was $30,700, although people in the north were, on average, wealthier than those in the south. In fact, more than 45 percent of the population in southern Italy lived in poverty

Ferrari, manufacturer of sports cars and sleek race cars, is based in Maranello, Italy.

CURRENCY OF ITALY

Italy's former currency was the lira. Its banknotes featured images of important Italians and Italian landmarks. Since 2002, Italy has used the currency of the EU, the euro.

Euro bills range from five to 500 euros and feature symbols of European unity—a map of Europe, the EU flag, and symbols such as arches, bridges, and gateways. Euro coins range from one cent to two euros. The front of each coin features a map of Europe; the reverse varies in each EU country. In Italy, the backs of the coins feature images from Italian art, architecture, and literature.

in 2009.[4] The country's generous welfare system, combined with strong family networks, helps people in poverty survive. Due to high unemployment and poverty, an underground or so-called black economy operates in the country. Income from the black market is not reported and not taxed, causing the government to lose revenue. In addition, organized crime operates using the black market.

Italy's economic struggles are caused, in large part, by mismanagement among government leaders. Issues include a staggering public debt that exceeds the GDP, corruption such as graft and special favors, and an imbalance in economic growth and development from the north to the south. Organized crime is also big business in Italy, making about 130 billion euros a year, or approximately 6 percent of the nation's GDP.[5] Although some Italian businesses have risen to the challenge

Italy's currency, the euro

of globalization, others are threatened by competition from foreign companies and, more recently, by immigration, as people come to Italy from China and other countries in search of work.

RESOURCES AND TRADE

Like many other members of the EU, Italy's currency is the euro. In 2011, approximately 0.7 euros were equal to one US dollar.

Italy has limited natural resources, but they include fish and some natural gas. Also of significant value is the country's legacy of quality in design and artistry. Many of the nation's industries are small businesses composed of artisans and craftspeople, and even the larger industries, such as the car manufacturer Ferrari and

MADE IN ITALY

Italian manufacturers realized in the 1980s that they could not compete with countries such as China on the price of goods—Chinese goods would always be cheaper. Instead, the Italians focused on building their reputation for quality. Clothing and accessories labeled "Made in Italy" were perceived as higher quality than goods from other nations. However, immigrants from China and other countries began setting up shop in Italy, producing cheaper and lower quality goods that technically deserved the "Made in Italy" label, staining the brand's high-end reputation. Some local government officials note that foreigner factory owners take the money they earn in Italy and return it to their own countries, removing the money from the Italian economy. Foreign factory owners argue that they are important job creators in Italian cities and serve an important market.

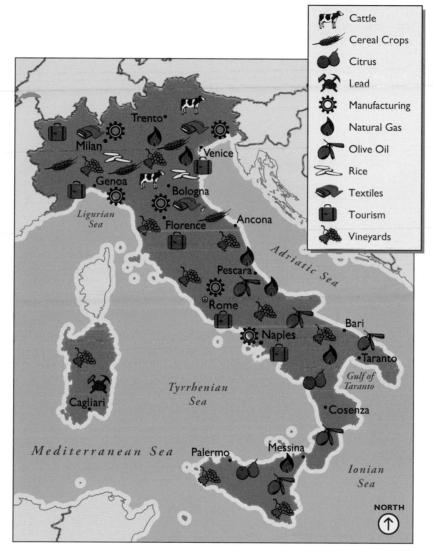

Legend:
- Cattle
- Cereal Crops
- Citrus
- Lead
- Manufacturing
- Natural Gas
- Olive Oil
- Rice
- Textiles
- Tourism
- Vineyards

Resources of Italy

PRODUCTS OF ITALIAN
INDUSTRY AND AGRICULTURE

Industries	Agriculture
Tourism, machinery, ceramics, chemicals, food processing, textiles, motor vehicles, clothing, footwear, and iron and steel	Fruits, vegetables, grapes, potatoes, sugar beets, soybeans, grain, olives, beef, dairy products, and fish

Italy's many renowned fashion houses, depend on design, artistry, and craftsmanship.

Before World War II, most of the Italian workforce labored in agricultural jobs. This changed after the war, however. By the year 2005, only 1.8 percent of the workforce was employed in agriculture, whereas 24.9 percent worked in industry and 73.3 percent worked in the service industry.[6]

Tourism is one of the service industries that is important to Italy. The World Travel and Tourism Council estimated that 45,392,000 tourists would come to the country in 2011.[7] The agency also estimated that tourism, including the money spent by visitors to Italy, was on the

Vineyards and olive farms still dot the Italian countryside.

rise. Revenues from tourism increased by 3.3 percent in 2010 to $1,770 billion.[8]

Italy makes and exports a variety of products, including engineering goods, metals, production machinery, motor vehicles, transport equipment, chemicals, food, beverages, tobacco, minerals, and textiles and clothing. It exports these products primarily to Europe and the United States. Specifically, Italy exports 12.60 percent of its products to Germany, 11.57 percent to France, 5.92 percent to the United States, 5.69 percent to Spain, 5.13 percent to the United Kingdom, and 4.69 percent to Switzerland.[9]

AN OUTSIZED NEED FOR FUEL

Italy's need for fuel far exceeds its ability to produce fuel. Italy is the fourth-largest importer of natural gas and the eleventh-largest importer of oil in the world.[10] It depends, in large part, on its Arab neighbor to the south, Libya, for oil. In 2010, 22 percent of Italy's oil came from Libya.[11]

Italy has limited fuel and imports a significant amount of the oil and gas needed for industry and transportation. It also imports engineering products, chemicals, transport equipment, energy products, food, beverages, tobacco, minerals and nonferrous metals, and textiles and clothing. Most Italian imports come from Europe and China.

Today, Italy faces three primary economic challenges. The first is to find more equitable ways to distribute income and economic opportunities from north to south. Other challenges are to reign in the public debt and to find alternatives to foreign fuel, increasing the nation's economic independence.

Italy ranks eighth in the world in total imports and in total exports.

CHAPTER 9
ITALY TODAY

Italy has historically been known for its warm culture, delicious cuisine, and artistic and historic legacies. Most Italians take time to savor food and to spend time with friends and family. As evidenced by the now internationally popular Slow Food movement, the Italian approach to life offers an alternative to the fast-paced and consumer-driven global culture of the twenty-first century.

Social ties and conversation are highly valued in Italy. The primary social unit is the family, but local and community relations are also important. In addition to sharing meals and conversation, Italians generally go out of their way to help family members get ahead and succeed— an approach that often extends to neighbors, friends, and community members.

At dinner, Italians will usually encourage their guests to take multiple servings.

Cuisine and dining continue to figure prominently in Italian life.

Even as the structure of the Italian family has changed, with women working outside the home and having fewer children than in previous times, family bonds have remained close. Young adults remain in their parents' homes longer, on average, than those in many other countries, extending social relations between adult children and their parents. Grandparents often live with the family or live nearby and assist with child care.

The Catholic Church continues to have an influence on the Italian family, but not to the extent that might be expected in a predominantly Catholic nation that has been the seat of the Roman Catholic Church for centuries. Marriage, a staple of family relations according to the church, has decreased in Italy, yet among Italian couples that do choose to marry, four out of five still do so in a church. And even though Italians voted to legalize divorce, it is still less common in Italy than other areas of Europe. Italy is often cited as having the lowest divorce rate in Europe.[1]

WEDDING BELLS

The number of marriages performed per 1,000 people in Italy dropped from 7.1 in 1950 to 5.4 in 1989, moving closer to the average number of marriages performed in other European countries.[2] Common law marriages, in which unmarried couples live together for many years, are increasing in Italy but are still less common than in the rest of Europe.

Religion has remained a pivotal part of society in modern day Italy, as witnessed by the crowd of attendees during Easter Mass at the Vatican.

TEEN LIFE

Italians' emphasis on family is important to Italian teens, as well. They enjoy time with family and tend to remain close with their parents. Boys, in particular, share a loving bond with their mothers.

Similar to teens worldwide, Italian teens enjoy spending time with friends, playing games and sports (especially soccer), and participating in popular culture, such as going to movies and listening to music. The Italian sense of style is as prevalent among teens as adults, but a US influence is also present, as shown by the popularity of blue jeans and rap music. Fast cars and mopeds are popular in Italy as well, particularly among young people. Teens who pass a test are allowed to drive a moped at age 14.

Teens' lives differ according to socioeconomic ties and region. Especially in the south of Italy, many teens are unemployed and thus susceptible to recruitment by gangs and organized crime.

TEENS AND DRINKING

Because of the cultural relationship among wine, food, and socializing, Italian teens often drink wine with family meals. But this custom does not seem to have led to an increase in alcohol abuse. In fact, Italian teens tend to look down on drunkenness, and they typically consider binge drinking, or drinking to excess, socially unacceptable. These views were confirmed in a 2003 survey by the European School Survey Project on Alcohol and Other Drugs, which found that drunkenness was less common among teens in Italy than in other European countries.[3]

Mobility and socializing are valued by Italian youth; many use mopeds to roam their cities and meet with friends.

SCHOOL ATTENDANCE AMONG ITALIANS

Preschool	Elementary and Middle School	High School	University or College
100 percent	98 percent (girls) 99 percent (boys)	95 percent (girls) 94 percent (boys)	67 percent[6]

EDUCATION

Italy has a high rate of literacy, as 98.4 percent of Italians aged 15 and older can read and write.[4] The average length of time spent in school is 16 years, and it includes elementary, middle, and high school.[5]

Children typically complete five years of primary school, three years of lower-secondary school (similar to middle school), and five years of upper-secondary school (similar to high school). Upper-secondary school offers options in programs ranging from a classical education, with an emphasis on humanities and some science courses, to technical school, with an emphasis on the arts, sciences, or language. After completing secondary school, most teens attend either a university program or an apprenticeship program, in which they learn a trade or a craft.

The first modern university was established in Bologna in the eleventh century, and today Italy is home to many internationally

Italian high school culminates in exams.

respected universities. Many universities are publicly funded, keeping tuition low. These public universities accept almost all applicants with high school diplomas. Private universities are also an option for Italian students.

ITALY TODAY AND TOMORROW

The challenges Italy faces today have persisted for much of the last century. Key problems include expanding opportunities from the north to the south, managing the large public debt, reducing corruption, reducing government spending, and controlling special interests in the centralized government. Italy also faces the challenge of curtailing the continued violence and influence of the nation's crime syndicates.

Addressing immigration to Italy is another recent challenge, as the nation tried to adjust to waves of new immigrants arriving from southeastern Europe and northern Africa. As more and more people have come to Italy, the country has struggled to make laws to fairly address immigration.

In 2009, Italy had more than 23 million Internet users, the thirteenth-most in the world.

The outlook for Italy will depend on how the nation's government adapts to the changing world economy and whether it can implement more efficient economic systems to cut back on debt and government spending. Even so, both large and small businesses seem likely to remain successful in turning out unique fashion and design, manufacturing high-quality goods, and serving the public.

Italians across the country called for Berlusconi's resignation in February 2011.

The Italian emphasis on maintaining social ties and enjoying life's basic pleasures, such as beauty and good food, represents a healthy alternative to the fast pace of contemporary society in other parts of the world. Italians will likely continue their long tradition of maintaining a sociable, passionate, and artistic culture, leading the world in finding grace and beauty in today's highly competitive and consumer-driven culture. Finally, the Italian tourism industry will surely continue to thrive, as people from across the globe travel to the home of a civilization that has had a profound influence on the Western world.

With a melding of contemporary culture, exquisite relics from a rich history, and a tightly-woven social and family life, Italy's future looks promising.

[TIMELINE]

2000 BCE	Peoples form and live in agricultural settlements in what is today Italy.
600s–300s BCE	The Etruscans flourish on the Italian Peninsula.
753 BCE	According to legend, Rome is founded by Romulus on the banks of the Tiber River.
31 BCE	Octavian defeats Antony and Cleopatra and claims Egypt for the Roman Empire.
312 CE	Roman emperor Constantine makes Christianity the official religion of the republic.
395	The weakened Roman Empire splits into two parts.
476	The last Roman emperor, Romulus Augustus, is defeated by German leader Odoacer.
750s–770s	Frankish King Charlemagne gains control over much of northern Italy.
900s–1000s	The Italian city-states grow powerful.
1400s–1500s	The arts flourish during the Renaissance.
1848	Italians fight to unite the country and gain independence from Austria.
1860	Giuseppe Garibaldi invades Sicily and takes control of southern Italy for the nation.

1861	The Kingdom of Italy is formed officially on March 17 and Victor Emmanuel II becomes king.
1915	Italy enters World War I on the side of the Allied powers.
1919	Benito Mussolini forms a fascist political party in Italy.
1922	Mussolini and his forces march on Rome and the king gives him power over the government.
1929	The Lateran Treaty establishes the Vatican as a sovereign state.
1940	Italy enters World War II on the side of Germany and the Nazis.
1943	King Victor Emmanuel III ousts Mussolini, and Italy surrenders to Allied forces.
1946	The Italian people vote to end the monarchy, and the Italian Republic is established.
1957	Italy and other European nations sign the Treaty of Rome, forming the European Economic Community.
2002	Italy's currency shifts from the lira to the euro.
2008	Silvio Berlusconi begins his third term as prime minister on May 8.
2009	On April 6, an earthquake strikes the Abruzzi region east of Rome, killing approximately 300 people and leaving at least 1,500 homeless.

[FACTS AT YOUR FINGERTIPS]

GEOGRAPHY

Official name: Italian Republic
(in Italian, Repubblica Italiana)

Area: 116,348 square miles
(301,340 sq km)

Climate: Warm and sunny with cool winters throughout most of the peninsula, cooler inland than on the coasts, cold and snowy in northern mountains.

Highest elevation: Mont Blanc de Courmayeur, 15,577 feet (4,748 m) above sea level

Lowest elevation: Mediterranean Sea, 0 feet (0 m) below sea level

Significant geographic features: Mount Vesuvius

PEOPLE

Population (July 2011 est.):
58,090,681

Most populous city: Rome

Ethnic groups: Italian; with small clusters of German Italians, French Italians, and Slovene Italians in the north and Albanian Italians and Greek Italians in the south

Percentage of residents living in urban areas: 68 percent

Life expectancy: 80.33 years at birth (world rank: 23)

Language: Italian

Religion(s): Roman Catholicism, 90 percent (approximately one-third practicing); other 10 percent includes Protestantism, Judaism, and Islam

GOVERNMENT AND ECONOMY

Government: republic

Capital: Rome

Date of adoption of current constitution: December 11,1947, effective January 1, 1948

Head of state: president

Head of government: prime minister

Legislature: Parliament, consists of Senate and Chamber of Deputies

Currency: euro

Industries and natural resources: Limited natural resources include fish and some natural gas. Italy has a tradition of craftsmanship, quality, and artistry that is evident in industries such as textiles, motor vehicles, clothing, footwear, and ceramics. Other industries include tourism, machinery, food processing, chemicals, and iron and steel.

NATIONAL SYMBOLS

Holidays: Republic Day, on June 2, is a national holiday. It celebrates the day in 1946 when the people voted to end the monarchy and establish a republic. Religious holidays include

Easter, Christmas, and numerous saints' days.

Flag: Three vertical bands: green, white, and red

National anthem: "Il Canto degli Italiani" ("The Song of the Italians")

National animal: Italian wolf (unofficial)

KEY PEOPLE

Augustus, born Octavian, (63 BCE–14 CE), one of Julius Caesar's two successors; defeated rival Mark Antony to secure the Roman Empire.

Leonardo da Vinci (1452–1519), painter, sculptor, architect, engineer, and scientist; one of the most influential artists and thinkers of the Italian Renaissance

Galileo Galilei (1564–1642), renowned astronomer and physicist; made numerous contributions to modern science, including the Copernican theory of the universe, which showed that Earth revolved around the sun

Federico Fellini (1920–1993), influential artistic filmmaker, who developed a personal and surrealist style

REGIONS OF ITALY

Region; Capital

Abruzzi; L'Aquila

Basilicata; Potenza

Calabria; Catanzaro

Campania; Naples

Emilia-Romangna; Bologna

Lazio (Latium); Rome

Liguria; Genoa

Lombardy; Milan

Marche; Ancona

Molise; Campobasso

Piedmont; Turin

Puglia; Bari

Tuscany; Florence

Umbria; Perugia

Veneto; Venice

Autonomous Region; Capital

Friuli–Venezia Giulia; Trieste

Sardinia; Cagliari

Sicily; Palermo

Trentino–Alto Adige; Trento

Valle d'Aosta; Aosta

[GLOSSARY]

anarchist

> A person who is against the rule of government and sometimes uses violent means to rebel against the power of authority.

Baroque

> A decorative style of art and architecture prevalent in the seventeenth century; characterized by bold ornamentation and a mixture of styles and forms.

city-state

> A sovereign or autonomous city and its surrounding territory.

dictatorship

> A form of government in which the power is concentrated in the hands of one person, a dictator or autocrat.

fascism

> A form of government that places the nation above the individual and in which power is concentrated in one individual leader; marked by excessive restriction of individuality and regimentation of society and economy.

fresco

> A type of painting done with water-based pigments on wet plaster.

gladiator

> A warrior in a battle to the death that provided a form of public entertainment in ancient Rome.

gondola

> A long, narrow boat with a high prow; used in the canals of Venice.

Gothic

A style of architecture that began in France in the twelfth century and became popular in Europe through the sixteenth century; characterized by pointed arches and a balance of slender verticals and flying buttresses, or supports.

graft

The illegal or dishonest taking of money for favors, especially in politics or the government.

republic

A government in which the leader is not a monarch but a political authority made up of a small group or a leader; often elected, at least in part, by the people.

Roman Catholic

The doctrine of Christianity defined by the Catholic Church with its base in the Vatican, a nation within the city of Rome.

Socialist

A person whose political beliefs are Socialist, referring to a range of sociopolitical theories in which the government owns all or part of the nation's resources and controls the production and distribution of goods.

sovereign

Independent or self-governing.

ADDITIONAL RESOURCES

SELECTED BIBLIOGRAPHY

Holmes, George. *The Oxford History of Italy*. Oxford, UK: Oxford UP, 1997. Print.

Killinger, Charles. *Culture and Customs of Italy*. Westport, CT: Greenwood, 2005. Print.

Simonis, Damien. *Lonely Planet: Italy*. Victoria, Austral.: Lonely Planet, 2010. Print.

FURTHER READINGS

Branch, Gregory. *Renaissance Artists Who Inspired the World*. Brea, CA: Ballard and Tighe, 2004.

James, Simon. *Ancient Rome*. New York: DK, 2008.

Kras, Sara Louise. *The Food of Italy*. New York: Benchmark, 2011.

WEB LINKS

To learn more about Italy, visit ABDO Publishing Company online at **www.abdopublishing.com**. Web sites about Italy are featured on our Book Links page. These links are routinely monitored and updated to provide the most current information available.

PLACES TO VISIT

If you are ever in Italy, consider checking out these important and interesting sites!

The Colosseum

Visit the heart of the ancient Roman Empire.

Il Duomo

Experience this architectural marvel in the heart of Florence.

Piazza San Marco

Enjoy an espresso and the view of Venice from this famed plaza lined with cafés.

[SOURCE NOTES]

CHAPTER 1. A VISIT TO ITALY

1. Michael Sheridan. *Romans: Their Lives and Times.* New York: St. Martin's, 1994. Print. 2.

2. Damien Simonis. *Lonely Planet: Italy.* Victoria, Austral.: Lonely Planet, 2010. Print. 112.

3. Dianne Hales. *La Bella Lingua: My Love Affair with Italian, the World's Most Enchanting Language.* New York: Broadway, 2009. Print. 179.

CHAPTER 2. GEOGRAPHY: FROM THE MOUNTAINS TO THE SEAS

1. "The World Factbook: Italy." Central Intelligence Agency. Central Intelligence Agency, 6 Apr. 2011. Web. 20 Apr. 2011.

2. Damien Simonis. *Lonely Planet: Italy.* Victoria, Austral.: Lonely Planet, 2010. Print. 81.

3. Ibid.

4. Ibid.

5. Erla Zwingle. "Po: River of Pain and Plenty." *National Geographic Magazine.* National Geographic Society, 2002. Web. 20 Apr. 2011.

6. "Italy's Earthquake History." *BBC News.* BBC, 31 Oct. 2002. Web. 20 Apr. 2011.

7. Ibid.

8. "Times Topics: L'Aquila Earthquake (2009)." *New York Times.* New York Times, n.d. Web. 20 Apr. 2011.

9. Damien Simonis. *Lonely Planet: Italy.* Victoria, Austral.: Lonely Planet, 2010. Print. 81.

10. "Venice and its Lagoon." *United Nations Educational, Scientific, and Cultural Organization: World Heritage Convention.* UNESCO World Heritage Center, n.d. Web. 20 Apr. 2011.

11. "Country Guide: Italy." *BBC: Weather.* BBC, n.d. Web. 14 Jan. 2011.

12. Ibid.

CHAPTER 3. ANIMALS AND NATURE: A THRIVING PENINSULA

1. "Italy's Wolves Bounce Back." *Physorg.com.* PhysOrg.com, 9 Feb. 2007. Web. 20 Apr. 2011.

2. "Summary Statistics: Summaries by Country, Table 5, Threatened Species in Each Country." *IUCN Red List of Threatened Species.* International Union for Conservation of Nature and Natural Resources, 2010. Web. 10 Feb. 2011.

3. Damien Simonis. *Lonely Planet: Italy*. Victoria, Austral.: Lonely Planet, 2010. Print. 84.

4. Ibid. 84.

5. Ibld. 86.

CHAPTER 4. HISTORY: AN INFLUENTIAL PAST

None.

CHAPTER 5. PEOPLE: GRACE AND STYLE

1. "The World Factbook: Italy." *Central Intelligence Agency*. Central Intelligence Agency, 6 Apr. 2011. Web. 20 Apr. 2011.

2. Ibid.

3. Ibid.

4. Ibid.

5. Ibid.

6. Ibid.

7. Ibid.

8. Ibid.

9. Damien Simonis. *Lonely Planet: Italy*. Victoria, Austral.: Lonely Planet, 2010. Print. 61.

10. Charles Killinger. *Culture and Customs of Italy*. Westport, CT: Greenwood, 2005. Print. 78.

11. Daniel Macleod. "Italian Mammas Making Offers Their Sons Can't Refuse." *Guardian. co.uk.* Guardian News and Media, 3 Feb. 2006. Web. 20 Apr. 2011.

CHAPTER 6. CULTURE: ART AND BEAUTY

1. Damien Simonis. *Lonely Planet: Italy*. Victoria, Austral.: Lonely Planet, 2010. Print. 73.

2. "European Heroes: Carlo Petrini; The Slow Revolutionary." *Time Europe*. Time, 2004. Web. 20 Apr. 2011.

3. "Rider Biographies: Alfredo Binda." *Cycling Hall of Fame*. Cycling Hall of Fame, n.d. Web. 20 Apr. 2011.

CHAPTER 7. POLITICS: MANY VOICES

1. "What Is the European Union?" *Europa: Panorama of the European Union*. European Union, n.d. Web. 20 Apr. 2011.

2. Ibid.

3. "On This Day—August 2. 1980: Bologna Blast Leaves Dozens Dead." *BBC News*. BBC, 2 Aug. 1980. Web 20 Apr. 2011.

4. Stephen Brown. "In Italy, Mafia May Be Winners as Economy Stalls." *USA Today*. USA Today, 11 Nov. 2008. Web. 20 Apr. 2011.

CHAPTER 8. ECONOMICS: THE STRENGTH OF FAMILIES

1. Charles Killinger. *Culture and Customs of Italy.* Westport, CT: Greenwood, 2005. Print. 72.

2. Ibid. 73.

3. "The World Factbook: Italy." *Central Intelligence Agency*. Central Intelligence Agency, 6 Apr. 2011. Web. 20 Apr. 2011.

4. "Italy: The Problem of Poverty as a Restriction on Access to Training and Employment." *EAEA News*. European Association for the Education of Adults, 23 Jan. 2010. Web. 8 May 2011.

5. "Mafia Boosted by Credit Crisis." *BBC News*. BBC, 12 Nov. 2008. Web. 20 Apr. 2011.

6. "The World Factbook: Italy." *Central Intelligence Agency*. Central Intelligence Agency, 6 Apr. 2011. Web. 20 Apr. 2011.

7. "Tourism Research: Economic Research: Country Reports: Italy." *Travel and Tourism Economic Impact 2011*. World Travel and Tourism Council, 2007. Web. 20 Apr. 2011.

8. Ibid.

9. "The World Factbook: Italy." *Central Intelligence Agency*. Central Intelligence Agency, 6 Apr. 2011. Web. 20 Apr. 2011.

10. Ibid.

11. Andrés Cala. "Europe Rethinks Dependence on Libyan Oil." *Christian Science Monitor*. Christian Science Monitor, 23 Feb. 2011. Web. 20 Apr. 2011.

CHAPTER 9. ITALY TODAY

1. Charles Killinger. *Culture and Customs of Italy.* Westport, CT: Greenwood, 2005. Print. 76.

2. Ibid.

3. "Italy." *European School Survey Project on Alcohol and Other Drugs.* ESPAD, 2007. Web. 20 Apr. 2011.

4. "The World Factbook: Italy." *Central Intelligence Agency.* Central Intelligence Agency, 6 Apr. 2011. Web. 20 Apr. 2011.

5. Ibid.

6. "UIS Statistics in Brief: Education in Italy." *UNESCO Institute for Statistics.* UNESCO, n.d. Web. 20 Apr. 2011.

[INDEX]

PHOTO CREDITS